meditation

meditation

a path to consciousness

merwede van der merwe

HUMAN & ROUSSEAU
Cape Town Pretoria Johannesburg

Copyright © 1997 by Merwede van der Merwe

First edition in 1997 by Human & Rousseau (Pty) Ltd
State House, 3-9 Rose Street, Cape Town
Typography and cover design by Chérie Collins
Cover photograph by Paul Alberts
Typeset in 12 on 16 pt Cloister
by Human & Rousseau
Printed and bound by National Book Printers,
Drukkery Street, Goodwood, Western Cape

ISBN 0 7981 3702 9

contents

a special thank you to paul alberts
for the use of his photographs

foreword

Human beings at various times in their history have been called upon to perform new acts of adaptation in order to adjust to changing circumstances.

To say that we live in times of enormous change has become trite, but never before has so much been demanded of us in our quest for survival. Everything around us is changing at a speed hitherto unheard of; not only do we not know what giant steps technology is going to take next, but we do not know what large-scale human tragedy we may face tomorrow.

The global village has brought everything closer and more immediate than before, with the result that we are forced either to escape into complete unconsciousness, chemically or culturally induced, or to dig up from deep within ourselves greater depths of spirituality than were ever previously demanded of us. Questions about ourselves, such as who we are, where we have come from and where we are heading have become critically pertinent.

One way in which men and women of great spirituality, over the ages, have succeeded in making contact with themselves is by means of meditation, a method of creating an inner space of calmness and reflection whereby we can confront the inner wisdom that we are all heir to. Today, more than ever, we need this place of centredness in our quest for understanding. This may be one of the few avenues open to us for staying in control of our lives, and not being overwhelmed by all the forces inside and outside us that tend to take over as the controlling forces in our lives.

If you are interested in acquiring this authentic power, then the outcome of Merwede van der Merwe's own quest, her own searching over the past number of years, will pave the way for an understanding of how we are, and should be, one undivided living unit of body and soul and spirit. Her journey from meditation to wisdom may assist you in taking authentic control over your own life.

AMPIE MULLER
Senior Consultant, Centre for Conflict Resolution, Cape Town

Professor Muller is a psychologist who over the years has had a great interest in the work of Carl Jung, and has tried to discover how Eastern insight can complement our own Western technology driven attemps at understanding ourselves and our relationships.

"Never in the history of the human race have the dangers been so extreme; yet in their role as evolutionary catalysts, they may be just what is needed to push us to a higher level."
– *Peter Russell*

"To take responsibility for what we do and do not do is to take power; to avoid responsibility is to make ourselves victims, objects."
– *James Bugental*

"What will bring human understanding and compassion is the recognition of our common ignorance and frailty, that there are no authorities with the right answers."
– *Jay Williams*

introduction

Meditation is an ancient technique for stilling the mind. Its aim is to open the mind to greater awareness in order to expand consciousness. Becoming more conscious of who we are and what we are doing on this planet is the natural curve of our evolution. Consciousness broadens our understanding. The greater our understanding of what we are doing, the clearer we can be about our responsibilities, both individually and collectively.

South Africa is going through profound transformation. We are changing our thinking; we are in the process of reinventing our world. The sociopolitical situation is forcing radical change on all levels of society. As the people of our country find new ways of sharing and living together, we are all discovering new realities, new truths.

The outer changes are igniting inner changes. Laws to enforce separateness have been replaced by the acknowledgement and acceptance of our interdependence. The universal truth of the interrelatedness of all life is slowly becoming part of our understanding of our world.

Living with awareness is a challenge. Living in South Africa in the 1990s is an experience which cannot be fully appreciated without awareness. Through awareness we gain insight, and insight cultivates greater understanding, greater acceptance. This is how we evolve and this is how we expand our consciousness. In the words of Gary Zukav: "If you choose unconsciously, you evolve unconsciously. If you choose consciously, you evolve consciously". The practice of meditation focuses directly and uniquely on this process. Through meditation the mind becomes still and awareness increases.

Meditation has never been part of the South African way of life. It is a practice that has mistakenly been associated with religion. Yet meditation is older and broader than any religious movement or dogma. In the East it has been used by different cultures in many different ways for centuries. In the West the tradition was first opposed, then forgotten and in recent times rediscovered.

This new interest in an ancient technique for mind training and inner development is growing in South Africa. We, like the rest of the world, are discovering that we need to find answers within ourselves. The New South Africa needs people with clear, sharp minds. We need people who can think widely and creatively; we need people who are fully conscious. Meditation is a powerful and simple technique for speeding up the process of mental evolution.

As we approach the turn of the century, new ways of evaluating our presence on this planet are emerging. As we discover and develop our abilities to evolve beyond dependency and beyond victim consciousness, we are becoming more cocreative with the universe. Values and perceptions are changing all the time and a new world-view is emerging. One of the most important aspects of this new vision is the issue of power.

The time has come, in South Africa as in the rest of the world, for us to become fully self-empowered human beings. A person who is self-empowered has the courage and the wisdom to follow inner authority.

External authority is the influence that the outside world has on us. It is the values and perceptions that we adopt from society, from others. Inner authority is the voice of our own truth, of our intuition. When we are governed by inner authority, we are authentically empowered human beings.

We are slowly learning that we cannot forever give our personal power to an outside authority. The government, the churches and the medical profession all have ways and means of trying to create a helpful and safe infrastructure for society to operate within. They create structures for society to function in a civilised way. They cannot and should not prescribe to us how to live our lives. Authority systems are there to establish order and bring support. They cannot feel or think on behalf of an individual.

We are traditionally a law-abiding and God-fearing country. We have been content to accept the authority of the President, the minister, the priest, the dominee and the medical doctor. The new worldview focuses on the need for individuals to develop and cultivate their own inner authority. Worldwide, people are finding it necessary to take greater responsibility for themselves and for their contribution to society and the wellbeing of the planet.

Most thinking people accept the concept that if you want to change the world you need to start with yourself. Greater awareness automatically extends one's ability to take responsibility for oneself. This need is especially great in South Africa. To build a new country, to live in harmony with each other, each of us needs to become more self-reliant and more empowered. Expanding one's consciousness means becoming a more authentically empowered human being. Meditation practice is a sure and solid way of cultivating authentic power.

In *The Seat of the Soul*, Gary Zukav explains beautifully how the evolution of our species is at present shifting from the pursuit of external power to the pursuit of authentic power. He writes: "Our deeper understanding leads us to another kind of power, a power that loves life in every form that it appears, a power that does not judge what it encounters . . . This is authentic power . . . When we align our thoughts, emotions and actions with the highest part of ourselves, we are filled with enthusiasm, purpose and meaning . . . This is the experience of authentic power. Authentic power has its roots in the deepest source of our being."

The future of South Africa does not depend on the wheeling and dealing of those people who manipulate external power. Politics, money and glamour will keep on changing hands in the years and centuries to come. The future of our country depends on how conscious our people can become; it depends on the cultivation of authentic power.

For South Africa, as for the rest of the world, the twenty-first century will be a time of discovering the universal truths of interrelatedness and interdependency. Each individual, group or community that expands in consciousness serves the whole. We all have a basic responsibility to develop ourselves, to become more aware, to cultivate authentic power. Meditation is a simple and safe tool to help us achieve this.

"Self-transformation is a *process*; it is not the sudden consequence of a mere resolution to change."
– *Kriyananda*

"The most essential purpose of the human adventure on earth is to become more than what one was born. It is to actualize, in a specific and concrete way, our potential."
– *Peter R. de Coppens*

"Through the practice of sitting still and following your breath as it goes out and dissolves, you are connecting with your heart. By simply letting yourself be, as you are, you develop genuine sympathy towards yourself."
– *Chögyam Trungpa*

"I do not know if you have ever noticed that when you give total attention there is complete silence. And in that attention there is no frontier, there is no centre, as the 'me' who is aware or attentive. That attention, that silence, is a state of meditation."
– *Krishnamurti*

"Meditation is synonymous with the practice of non-doing."
– *Jon Kabat-Zinn*

"Everything is done by the mind except meditation. Because meditation is not an achievement – it is already the case, it is your nature. It has not to be achieved; it has only to be recognized, it has only to be remembered."
– *Osho*

meditation

Meditation is stilling – the stilling of the mind through a process of concentration and inner focus. It is quite simply a process of drawing our full awareness into the self in order for the mind to come to a still point. The body is totally relaxed, one's breathing is quiet and the mind is gradually trained to become calm and focused.

The practice of meditation is a technique and the state of meditation is one of being in total awareness. This is a state which naturally allows consciousness to expand.

Through the ages many different meditation techniques have been developed. These provide different methods to people with particular needs and visions. The final goal is the same in all traditions: to bring that which is not conscious into consciousness. It is a process of expanding awareness, of realising dormant potential. Psychologists talk of self-actualisation, spiritual traditions speak of enlightenment.

Awareness and stillness are two of the most powerful tools for transforming consciousness. Through awareness we gain insight, and stillness helps us to centre ourselves. These are qualities which contribute directly towards our growth.

Meditation is thus a tool for self-development; it is a way of becoming more than we already are. At first it is a path to greater self-awareness. Later it becomes a way of expanding awareness beyond the self, to reach levels of transpersonal consciousness. Meditation is like growth, it never ends; it never reaches a point of final achievement.

It gently keeps on unfolding our inner potential.

Our natural progression through life is from infancy to adulthood, from immaturity to maturity, from unconsciousness to greater consciousness. This is our life purpose: to grow and to become more whole. We all go through this process automatically, but much of what happens along the way does not penetrate our awareness. We often experience ourselves as less than we are and we respond to life in a limited way. Through the process of meditation we learn how to live in the present moment with more awareness. We become more alive, and we grow in self-fulfilment.

The most popular technique for practising meditation is to sit down quietly, to relax the body, and to bring the mind to calmness through a simple concentration technique. Meditation can best be described as inner listening and nondoing. When we sit in stillness, the normal outside stimuli that we respond to are temporarily cut off and we discover the ability to turn our awareness inward. Inward focus stimulates inner listening.

Nondoing is an important part of the process, because awareness needs to unfold on its own; we cannot make it happen. Our contribution to the process is to practise a technique of concentration, such as focusing our attention on our breathing, which allows the mind to settle down and to become calm and centred.

We cannot do meditation, we use techniques to bring the mind into focus and we allow the state of meditation to unfold naturally.

"Be still – and know that I am God."
– *Psalm 46:10*

"If you love truth, be a lover of silence. Silence will unite you to God Himself. Love silence above everything else, for it brings a fruit the tongue is too feeble to describe."
– *St Isaac of Syria*

"Becoming silent and still, we know God without knowing, see God without seeing. There is darkness yet there is light. There is emptiness yet there is fullness."
– *Frank X. Tuoti*

"Many have entered the Kingdom without the sacraments. None has entered without prayer."
– *Karl Rahner*

"Contemplative prayer is the world in which God can do anything. To move into that realm is the greatest adventure. It is to be open to the Infinite and hence to infinite possibilities."
– *Thomas Keating*

"In prayer, more is accomplished by listening than by talking. Let us leave to God the decision as to what shall be said. God speaks to the heart only when the heart is recollected."
– *St Jane Chantal*

"The deepest level of communication is not communication, but communion. It is wordless. It is beyond words and it is beyond speech and beyond concepts."
– *Thomas Merton*

prayer

When we pray, we consciously enter into a relationship with God. We withdraw our senses from the outside world; we become still, and we enter into God's presence. This is the most important difference between prayer and meditation: when praying, we relate to God, when meditating, we still the discursive mind and we allow its natural state of quiet spaciousness to unfold.

Deep prayer is always a unique experience. Each time we enter into a relationship with God, we experience it in a different way, because prayer, like meditation, is an inner activity that always reflects our personal state of mind. Therefore, a settled, clear mind is as beneficial in prayer as it is in meditation. This is one of the most important similarities between prayer and meditation.

There are three classical stages of prayer. Vocal prayer, whether silent or said aloud, is when we speak to God. Discursive prayer is when we think about God, and contemplative prayer is when we rest in God. During contemplative prayer, we are silent in the presence of God; we do not come to God with an agenda; we simply open ourselves and we listen. The transformative power of prayer lies in this openness, this receptivity.

Since the days of the early Church Fathers, the root of prayer has been interior silence. For the first sixteen centuries of Christian faith, contemplative prayer was a powerful spiritual practice. Lost after the Reformation, the recovery of the Christian contemplative tradition

21

begun in the 1970s in the United States. An ancient contemplative practice, centring prayer, was reintroduced and has since spread to most parts of the Western world.

Centring prayer has much in common with mindfulness meditation. The techniques are similar and the aim of both practices is to cultivate greater awareness. The purpose of centring prayer is to awaken higher levels of consciousness, and to cultivate total openness to God. The aim is to move from ordinary awareness to spiritual awareness, to eventually gain access to the true self and then, finally, to dwell in the Divine Presence, the source of our being. For Westerners who feel drawn to the quiet state of meditation, centring prayer is an excellent way to make God the focus of one's meditation.

This method of praying is often referred to as "divine psychotherapy" because its aim is to break through the ego barriers which tend to block the transforming action of the indwelling presence of God. In the East the vision of the Divine is different to that in the West, but the purifying presence of "divine" psychotherapy, of releasing psychological blockages, is equally powerful in most methods of meditation.

Both centring prayer and meditation have gained recognition and great popularity during the last two decades. Both are methods for turning inward, for centring, for expanding consciousness. One method satisfies those who have religious needs, the other method is for those who prefer a secular method. Both methods work towards opening the mind and opening the heart, and then bringing the heart and mind into alignment. This is the path to love and wisdom, this is the path to Truth.

"Becoming an aware human being is a full time job . . . to choose a path of awareness is not an intellectual exercise. It is a living, breathing, constant discipline."
– *Caroline Myss*

"If we are to grasp the reality of our life while we have it, we will need to wake up to our moments. Otherwise, whole days, even a whole life, could slip past unnoticed."
– *Jon Kabat-Zinn*

"Awareness, awareness, awareness! In awareness is healing; in awareness is truth; in awareness is salvation; in awareness is spirituality; in awareness is growth; in awareness is love; in awareness is awakening. Awareness."
– *Anthony de Mello*

awareness

Awareness means being present in the moment. It means having direct contact with the moment-to-moment experiences of our lives. The senses are present, the mind is alert, and the intuition is awake. When we are fully aware, we are fully alive. We are absorbing, we are responding, we are understanding.

When we cultivate the quality of awareness through meditation, we are training the mind to be here, now. Most of the time our minds are preoccupied with past events or plans for the future. With awareness we learn to focus more on the present moment. When all our senses and our mind are focused on one place, our perception becomes sharp and clear.

A laser beam is the power of synchronised light. The power of a concentrated mind is much like laser light. Laser beams can cut or weld with great accuracy. They can cut through materials of all kinds with total precision. A clear and focused mind allows us to perceive reality as it is; it cuts through the layers of emotional fantasy.

Wisdom and truth are available to all people. At the source of all life there is truth. Wisdom is our human way of accessing this truth. A laser-sharp mind will find wisdom and truth just as naturally as a laser beam will strike its target.

Only when we focus our attention can we connect with the fullness of the moment. The surfboard champion, the conductor of a symphony orchestra, the pilot landing his plane, are all fully present in the moment. They need all their energies focused in one place in order to achieve their goals. When we start cultivating awareness, we are bringing ourselves more and more into the centre. We become more alive, more effective, and more responsible for our decisions and choices.

Awareness is not the same as thought. It is beyond thinking. It relates to consciousness, while thinking relates to the mind. Meditation sharpens awareness in a holistic way. The nature of meditation is such that it enhances physical, emotional and mental awareness. Spiritual awareness naturally unfolds during this process. Through awareness, we evolve as integrated human beings. It helps us to find the balance between the different parts that make up the wholeness of who we are.

We develop insight through awareness. This is how we grow in understanding and through understanding we move into self-acceptance. This is how we mature, this is the foundation of growing up: learning to accept ourselves and others. The insight that grows out of awareness helps us to become conscious of our mind games, our immature patterns and our unfinished business.

Seeing clearly enables us to let go of perceptions that are distorting our view of life. It enables us to change our attitude about something or someone when we are being judgemental. Without insight we cannot grow because we cannot see clearly.

Meditation is a path that leads to clearer vision. Regular practice cultivates inner vision as well as a sharper and more balanced vision of the external world.

AWARENESS OF THOUGHTS

It is important to become aware of the activity of the mind. To notice our thoughts is a preliminary step towards meditation. Just watching the movement of our thoughts is the first step to gaining insight. We must be aware of our thinking process if we want to gain some control over it.

1 Make yourself comfortable in a place where there are minimal outside stimuli. Settle your body. Relax and become aware of your breathing. Close your eyes.

2 Sit quietly and focus inward. Feel your body. Feel the movement in your chest.

3 Thoughts will rise up in your mind. Allow this to happen with an attitude of detachment. Remain an observer. Just simply note what you are thinking.

4 If you do not engage with the thoughts, they will come and go. Allow them to move in and out of your field of focus. Notice the type of thought. Name it to yourself: planning, remembering, worrying, imagining, criticising, fantasising . . .

5 Remain objective. Be aware of when you are starting to participate in the thought. Let go when you
   notice this happening. Return to simply observing.

6 When you get pulled into an obsessive thought,
   focus on your breathing. Take a couple of slow,
   deep breaths. Feel your chest expand. Feel your
   chest contract. Release the breath. Feel your body.
   Check that it is relaxed.

7 Sit quietly. Notice the next thought that arises.
   Name the thought. Sit quietly. Notice the next
   thought. Name it.

8 Continue watching your thoughts for at least five
   minutes at a time. Allow the process to happen
   without any judgement or interference. Just watch.

Mindwatching is a simple method of starting to
become aware of the activities of the mind. It focuses awareness on the moment and it introduces objectivity and detachment. It is a simple technique which
can be done several times each day.

growth

The process of evolution involves becoming more, more whole. It is a continual process, spiralling outward, or upward toward greater wholeness. When we throw a pebble into a still pond, there is at first a little splash, and then circles form, moving outward and becoming larger, increasing in the process. As we allow our awareness to keep moving outward, to keep expanding, reaching towards the beyond, we are opening up our consciousness.

Psychology and spirituality both engage this process. The former concerns itself with the here and now, the latter with the beyond. Psychology focuses on the personality; it deals with the world of the ego, all the needs, wants and games that are created by the ego in order to survive the here and the now. Spirituality focuses on the soul; it concerns itself with the world of spirit, opening up all the connecting routes between our spiritual awareness and the beyond.

Psychology is the path of integration, while spirituality is the path of purification. Both paths serve our evolution. We become more whole through integrating our personality and through aligning ourselves more and more with our soul.

Through meditation we open up awareness of these processes and our practice allows us to become more conscious of our own responsibility towards our journey of self-development. Meditation will bring up the suppressed and denied parts of our personalities, because the technique of meditation cultivates awareness and insight. By focusing

"Meditation *is* evolution; it *is* transformation – there is nothing really special about it. It seems quite mysterious and convoluted to the ego because it is development beyond the ego."
– *Ken Wilber*

"Once you accept the journey to become whole, to become an elegant spirit, you cannot go backwards. You cannot become 'unaware' ever again."
– *Caroline Myss*

"As far as we can discern, the sole purpose of human existence is to kindle a light in the darkness of mere being."
– *Carl Jung*

"Who and what we are is a part of how we see the world. Our identity is not a given but a continual creation-discovery."
– *James Bugental*

"You can only change through awareness and understanding . . . What you do not understand and are not aware of, you repress."
– *Anthony de Mello*

"The holistic evolution of nature shows up in the human psyche as development or growth. Psychological growth in humans is a microcosmic reflection of the universal growth. It has the same goals: the unfolding of ever higher unities of integrations. The whole of each level becomes a part of the whole of the next level."
– *Ken Wilber*

inward, we bring to consciousness that which is subconscious.

Meditation helps us to confront and accept our shadow – the dark side of our psyche which we tend to suppress or deny. In this way meditation assists us with the integration process of psychology. It should not replace psychology, but it should be seen as a method contributing to our process of individuation. Integrating the personality is one part of our life's journey. The other part concerns the beyond, and it is a journey of spiritual awareness, of discovering our interrelatedness with the universe.

Through our life force, our breathing, our inner essence, our spirit, we are connected to the universe. Our bodies are separate but our spirit is one. This is what all religions, philosophies and schools of wisdom try to explain: how do we as individuals relate to the macrocosmos? How do we relate to the universe and to the creative force that binds us all together? How do we relate to God?

This is where meditation differs from religion. Meditation has no answers, no dogma, no teaching. It is a process of bringing greater clarity to the mind through the process of purification. It brings us in contact with our inner knowledge, our intuition, our inner wisdom.

Meditation helps us to understand that the answers do not come from an outside authority, but that the truth resides within ourselves. Teachings can point the way, but we have to evolve towards finding our own inner truth. This is the path of spirituality, when we go beyond psychology, beyond the ego, when we find our connection with the rest of creation.

Meditation is a path of integration as well as purification. This is why meditation is the most dynamic tool for expanding consciousness; it serves the personality as well as the soul. When we practise meditation we are moving towards wholeness.

"When we inhale, the air comes into the inner world. When we exhale, the air goes out to the outer world. The inner world is limitless, and the outer world is also limitless. We say 'inner world' or 'outer world', but actually there is only one whole world."
– *Shunryu Suzuki*

"We should just try to keep our mind on our breathing. That is our actual practice. That effort will be refined more and more while you are sitting. At first the effort you make is quite rough and impure, but by the power of practice the effort will become purer and purer. When your effort becomes pure, your body and mind become pure."
– *Shunryu Suzuki*

"Every moment of conscious breath is an inspired co-creation with life itself."
– *Michael Sky*

breathing

Breathing forms the bridge between the body and the mind. When one's breathing is deep, regular and calm, the body and mind respond automatically. Breath awareness is an integral part of many stress-management programmes. Yogis have used breath manipulation as a tool to change consciousness for thousands of years. In the West we have only recently discovered the power of our own breathing.

Most people use only their upper chests when they breathe and are not aware of diaphragmatic breathing. Chest breathing is a shallow, ineffective way of breathing and it is the result of tightness in the chest and in the diaphragm. The benefits we get from changing our breathing pattern from chest breathing to diaphragmatic breathing are enormous.

The breath functions either voluntarily or involuntarily. We can wilfully control the flow of our breathing. This enables us to influence the functioning of our autonomic nervous system directly. Smooth, even breathing is the natural way for the body to breathe; this is how we were designed to breathe: using our diaphragms in a rhythmical, relaxed way.

Deep, regular, diaphragmatic breathing evokes the relaxation response: the heart rate decreases, the blood pressure drops, the metabolism slows down, the muscles relax, the brain waves shift from an alert beta rhythm to a relaxed alpha rhythm.

The foundation of all meditation techniques is to assist us in

releasing tightness in the mind and in the body. We cannot open ourselves to greater consciousness if we are holding on tightly to thoughts and muscles. Learning to let go of the tightness in the diaphragm and the chest is an excellent foundation for our meditation practice.

When we focus our attention on our breathing, we are in present time, we are attentive from moment to moment. There is an inhalation, an exhalation, and a pause in between. It is very simple just to pay attention to the way we are breathing – calmly watching the movement with full awareness.

However, to do this for a few minutes without thoughts intruding is very difficult because the mind is habitually busy all the time. This is why the technique of breath watching is so common in meditation practice, since it trains the mind in a natural and practical way.

Once we have introduced breath awareness into our lives, we have a tool that we can use at all times and in any place or circumstance. Through meditation practice we learn that our breathing is our best friend; it is our permanent companion and it is a direct way to expand our awareness.

As we become more acquainted with our breathing, we become aware of how miraculously we are linked to the universe, to life. When we are breathing, we are taking in life force, we are participating in life, we are alive. When we stop breathing, we die, we move on, but while we are here, we breathe all the time. Our breathing is our inner rhythm which connects us to the rhythm of the universe.

DIAPHRAGMATIC BREATHING

Deep, full breathing requires us to use the diaphragm with awareness and control. The diaphragm is also called the breathing muscle. When we use this muscle correctly, we directly influence the autonomic nervous system. We release tightness in the chest, we calm the mind, we centre our awareness.

1 Lie on your back on a flat surface. Your spine must be straight, your body warm and comfortable.

2 Your legs should be slightly apart, your feet relaxed and flopping outward.

3 Your arms should be slightly away from your body, palms facing upwards.

4 Release your jaw. Allow your eyes to close gently.

5 Let go of your whole body. Allow yourself just simply to sink into the earth.

6 Place your right hand above your navel, on your solar plexus. Your fingers should be apart and relaxed.

7   Place your left hand on your breastbone, with your fingers apart and relaxed.

8   Breathe slowly into the bottom part of your lungs. Let your diaphragm expand like a big baloon. Your right hand will rise as your solar plexus extends.

9   Your left hand and upper chest should not move.

10 As you breathe out, your solar plexus will fall.

11 Inhale to the count of 4, allowing your right hand to rise as your diaphragm expands.

12 Exhale to the count of 4, allowing your right hand to fall. The breath should flow out smoothly.

13 When you feel that your diaphragm is moving effortlessly, place your hands back on the floor.

14 Continue breathing deeply and rhythmically for five to ten minutes. Allow your body to relax completely. Pay attention to the sensations in your body as your chest expands and contracts.

This technique can be used before meditation to calm the body and the mind. It opens the chest and allows the whole body to relax and release tightness.

AWARENESS OF BREATHING

Using breathing as an object for focusing the mind is a common practice in most meditation traditions. Breath awareness anchors the mind in the present moment. It is an effective way to prepare the body and the mind for meditation.

1 Find a quiet, comfortable place to sit. Your spine must be straight, your chest open, your body relaxed.

2 Close your eyes gently. Take a few moments to centre your awareness in your body. Feel your body. Relax and let go of any tightness. Notice your breathing.

3 Take a few deep, slow breaths. Notice the movement of your diaphragm and chest.

4 Allow your breathing to come back to a natural rhythm. Pay attention to your breathing. Notice the inhalations and the exhalations. Discover the difference between them.

5 Sit for a few minutes and attentively watch your breathing. Keep your awareness focused in one place, either at the tip of your nose, or on the rising and falling of your chest or diaphragm.

6   Do not control or manipulate your breathing. Remain an objective observer. Notice how the rhythm gradually changes. Pay attention to the quality of your breathing: smoothness, depth, durations of in- and out-breaths.

7   Notice if there is a pause between the exhalation and the next inhalation. Remain aware of the duration of the pauses.

8   After a few minutes of observing, take a few slow, deep breaths again. Fill your lungs to capacity. Exhale completely after each in-breath. Feel your chest expanding and contracting. Pay attention to the flow of your breathing.

9   Return to natural breathing. Again simply be aware of your breathing taking place by itself. Notice the inhalations, the exhalations, the pause in between. Just watch. Continue for a few minutes.

10 Open your eyes, feel your body, reflect for a while and continue your activities.

This exercise can also be done at any time during the day. It focuses you in the present moment. It is a technique for centring and calming.

"Our body and mind are not two and not one. If you think your body and mind are two, that is wrong; if you think that they are one, that is also wrong. Our body and mind are both two *and* one."
– *Shunryu Suzuki*

"Psychological growth without body consciousness appears like a tree without roots."
– *Arnold Mindell*

"Your consciousness affects every cell in your body, and every cell in your body affects your consciousness. There is a mutuality."
– *Gary Zukav*

"To get inside the body and know what you are feeling, is the beginning of honesty."
– *Barry Long*

"The body is the soul presented in its richest and most expressive form. In the body, we see the soul articulated . . .
When we relate to our bodies as having soul, we attend to their beauty, their poetry and their expressiveness."
– *Thomas Moore*

"Your body is a spiritual tool. Appreciate the miracle that it is."
– *Swami Rhada*

"If you look after the root of the tree, the fragrance and flowering will come by itself. If you look after the body, the fragrance of the mind and spirit will come of itself."
– *B.K.S. Iyengar*

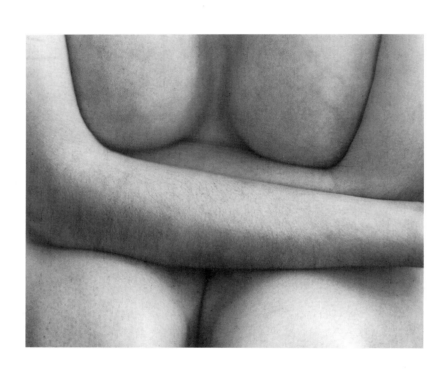

the body

The mind and the body are intimately linked. They support each other, stimulate each other and directly influence each other. Their interdependence demands that we pay attention to how they relate to each other.

If the mind is tense, the body will manifest that tension in tightness, discomfort or pain. If the mind is calm and peaceful, the body will be relaxed. When the body is tight with blocked energy, there will be an adverse effect on the mind. These interactions usually happen at an unconscious level, but they are very real nevertheless.

A body that is in good condition will contribute to the quality of our practice of meditation, while an unfit and unhealthy body will become a distraction during meditation. Life is a process of continual change and this is true for our physical condition as well. Some days we will be more sensitive to our body sensations than others. Paying attention to these changes is part of the training in awareness and acceptance.

The body is our vehicle within which we move through life; it is also the interpreter of our reality. We have five senses in order to see, hear, taste, smell and feel. This is how we read our world. Our sensual perceptions are interpreted by our mind and we respond with our emotions accordingly. This is how we create the experiences of our personal reality.

What we experience through our senses is what we believe our reality to be. When the sun is shining we can see the brightness around us, we can feel the warmth, we can hear the cicadas – we know it is a warm and sunny day. The brighter our senses, the brighter our reality; the duller our senses, the duller our reality. Some days we experience the sun as radiant, on other days we do not even hear the cicadas.

If the body is healthy, open and receptive, our sense perceptions will be clear and we will be more sensitive and appreciative of life. Body and mind are interdependent; the clarity of the senses is as important as the clarity of the mind.

Meditation influences the way we experience our outer as well as our inner realities, our physical relationship with the world as well as our nonphysical relationship. Our nonphysical world is the world of intuition, of sensing, inner knowledge and inspiration. These senses are as dependent on purity of body and clarity of mind as the other five senses. When we want to develop our interaction with the world beyond the five senses, meditation will stand us in good stead.

Whether we practise meditation for relaxation or to unfold our intuition, the path to the mind is through the body. We cannot bypass the body, it is our vehicle. It is what holds us to the force of gravity, it is where we experience our feelings.

Our body is our first level of self-knowledge and self-acceptance. By honouring our body, we are honouring the manifestation of who we are. We are more than our bodies, much more. But the path of discovery starts with the body.

AWARENESS OF THE BODY

Becoming aware of one's body is an easy and practical way of focusing attention on the moment. The body is here now. All sensations are in present time. Scanning the body with awareness is a method of keeping the mind fully present. In the tradition of meditation this is called mindfulness.

1 Find a place where you can be quiet and private. Get into a comfortable standing position. If you are not wearing flat shoes, take off your shoes. Feel the ground under your feet.

2 Close your eyes gently. Bring your awareness into your body. Feel your body. Notice your balance.

3 Become aware of how you are breathing. Notice the inhalations and the exhalations. Become aware of the slight movement of your diaphragm.

4 Release and relax your jaw. Relax your face. Feel the balance of your head on your neck.

5 Relax your shoulders. Feel the weight of your arms and hands. Be aware of your breathing.

6 Let go completely of your abdominal area. Allow your tummy to become soft. Notice your breathing.

7 Be aware of your whole body. Notice the stillness. Feel the weight of your body. Release your weight completely. Allow it to move down your body and release into the ground. Let go of any holding on.

8 Focus your awareness on the crown of your head. Stretch it up towards the sky, allowing the spine to lenghthen. Your chest will open. Notice your length. Feel your breath moving.

9 Be fully aware of your whole body exactly as you are standing: its stillness, its balance, its weight, your feet on the ground, your breathing.

10 Now scan your body for sensations. Concentrate on each area and try to become aware of what you are feeling: softness, tingling, tightness.

11 Take a deep breath. Hold it for as long as you can. Be aware of your expanded chest. Release your breath slowly.

12 Scan your body again. Feel all the sensations.

With practice awareness will grow. You will start to notice more sensations in your body.

energy

Nothing in the universe is still. Subatomic particles are continually moving in symmetrical, rhythmical patterns. These vibratory patterns are the essence of all life. Since Einstein's special theory of relativity we have understood that energy and mass are different forms of the same thing.

Vibrating energy is what holds the universe together at a deep and fundamental level. What we see, feel, hear, and smell are all different forms of energy. When we walk, run, speak, or think, we are engaging different forms of energy. It is with our five senses that we relate to energy in the physical world and it is with our extrasensory perceptions, like intuition, that we relate to the energy patterns of the nonphysical world.

Through meditation we bring about transformation: we release stress from the body, we purify the mind, we open the heart, we expand consciousness. There is nothing mystical or weird about this. We are simply using the technique of meditation to change the vibratory quality of our energy fields.

The human energy field is sometimes referred to as an aura, sometimes as an electromagnetic field, sometimes as subtle energy bodies. Our physical body is interpenetrated and surrounded by this field of subtle energy which most of us cannot see with our ordinary eyes. Through technology, such as Kirlian photography, we can capture the vibratory quality of some of these fields. Individuals with highly developed intuitive or psychic abilities can see or feel these subtle energy fields.

We can refine the vibratory quality of our energy system through personal effort. When we have a more relaxed and healthy body, we experience ourselves and our world in a more balanced way. When we have greater clarity of mind, we have greater mental power. When our hearts are open, we experience compassion. This is how we transform ourselves, by refining our physical, mental and emotional energies.

Through fresh, wholesome food and exercise we contribute to the quality of our physical energies. Through body therapies like shiatsu, aromatherapy and the different body alignment methods that are available, we unblock the emotional and mental energies that are held within the physical body. With body-mind practices such as yoga and t'ai chi we align our physical and mental energies. This is how we lay a healthy and strong foundation. And then, through meditation, we endeavour to refine the energies of our consciousness.

We experience ourselves and our world through our energy field. Our senses monitor and our brain interprets, but the energetic experience is what we perceive as our "reality". When we change the vibratory quality of our energy field, we change the way we experience reality. The higher the vibrations, the finer the consciousness. This is the process of meditation.

"The sub-atomic realm is beyond the limits of sensory perception. It is also beyond the limits of rational understanding."
– Gary Zukav

"If Bohm's physics, or one similar to it, should become the main thrust of physics in the future, the dances of East and West could blend in exquisite harmony. It is possible that physics curricula of the twenty-first century will include classes in meditation."
– Gary Zukav

"In the East there never has been much philosophical or religious confusion about matter and energy . . . The way it really is cannot be communicated verbally, but in the attempt to talk about it, eastern literature speaks repeatedly of dancing energy and transient, impermanent forms. This is strikingly similar to the picture of physical reality emerging from high-energy particle physics."
– Gary Zukav

"Once you realize your own inner energy and learn to let it guide you, it will change your life forever."
– Richard M. Chin

"The energy that exists within the universe is the same energy that exists within ourselves."
– Richard M. Chin

"In your daily life, you should also be aware of your posture, your head and shoulders, how you walk, and how you look at people. Even when you are not meditating, you can maintain a dignified state of existence. You can transcend your embarrassment and take pride in being a human being. Such pride is acceptable and good."
– *Chögyam Trungpa*

"Extension brings space, space brings freedom, freedom brings precision. Precision is truth and truth is God."
– *B.K.S. Iyengar*

"The most important point is to own your physical body. If you slump, you will lose your self. Your mind will be wandering about somewhere else; you will not be in your body. This is not the way. We must exist right here, right now!"
– *Shunryu Suzuki*

posture

Traditionally meditators sit cross-legged on the ground. This is an Eastern tradition that often does not work for Westerners because our bodies are normally less supple. The important thing about the sitting posture is to keep the spine straight and the cross-legged position allows this to happen effortlessly.

When sitting on a cushion with crossed legs the knees should be lower than the sitting bones. This allows a slight forward tilt of the lumbar spine. This position gives optimum support to the upper body and allows the spine to be held erect with minimum or no effort.

To elongate the spine, we stretch gently upwards. Focusing on the crown of the head and lifting it up towards the ceiling is an effective way of lengthening the spine. The chest will open at the same time. The chin should be dropped down slightly.

The reason why so much emphasis is placed on the erect spine is because this position stimulates wakefulness and alertness. The spine's verticality cultivates awareness and allows the free flow of energy. One's physical posture influences the movement of energy in the torso as well as in the subtle energy bodies. Allowing the free flow of energy is a very important aspect of our practice.

When we slump, we allow the body to collapse into itself and this blocks the energy flow.

It is important for the body to be open and for us to be alert. We should feel no unnecessary discomfort. Our focus should be on con-

centrating the mind, not forcing or fighting the body. The body should assist us in our practice so it is important that we experiment and find a way of sitting that is effective. We want to be able to relax the body completely without slumping. This requires a sense of settledness and effortless balance.

An alternative to the cushion is a low stool which lifts the sitting bones and allows the meditator to tuck his or her feet under it. In the beginning we may, however, choose to sit on a bench or a straight-backed chair if the other positions cause discomfort.

Relaxing the jaw and shoulders and letting go of the stomach is part of settling into the posture. We are often unconscious of the fact that we are tight in these areas. When we sit down for our practice, we should pay attention to these areas and wilfully release any tightness.

Finding our posture and holding it for the duration of our practice is part of the training in awareness. Like our breathing, our bodies focus us in the moment because body sensations are in the present moment. Our bodies, more than our minds, help us to be here now.

We end our preparation by gently closing your eyes. When the eyes are closed we turn our gaze inward and we begin working with our chosen technique.

ALTERNATE NOSTRIL BREATHING

This is a centring technique which helps to develop the skill of concentration. It is important to keep your mind gently focused on your breathing. If your mind is anchored on the movement of your breathing, there will be no thoughts. The mind cannot do two things at the same time.

1   Sit in a comfortable position with your spine straight. Allow your head to balance effortlessly. Relax your jaw.

2   Close your eyes gently. Breathe through both nostrils until the inhalations and exhalations are smooth and of equal duration.

3   Bring your right hand up to your nose. Gently rest the tip of your thumb against the side of your right nostril.

4   Close off your right nostril and exhale through your left nostril.

5   Breathe in through your left nostril to the count of 4. At the end of the inhalation, close your left nostril by pressing gently against it with your ring finger.

6 Remove your thumb from your right nostril and exhale to the count of 4.

7 At the end of the exhalation breathe in through the same nostril to the count of 4.

8 Close your right nostril with your thumb, open your left nostril and exhale to the count of 4.

9 Repeat this cycle for 5 to 10 minutes, focusing your awareness on the movement of your breathing. Feel the sensations in your nose as the breath flows through.

10 There should be no forcing, no discomfort, no effort. Your breathing should be smooth, regular and flowing. Both nostrils must be open for this exercise.

This simple breathing technique prepares the body and mind for meditation. It centres awareness, balances left-right brain activity, and calms the autonomic nervous system and thus the whole body.

STILLING AND CENTRING

This is a basic preparation for sitting meditation. It is a method used to still the mind and to centre awareness. It is advisable to spend five or ten minutes in preparation before applying a technique of concentration.

1 Sit in a comfortable position with a straight spine, your hands on your lap, relaxed, palms upwards. Relax your body. Close your eyes. Be aware of your breathing.

2 Focus your awareness inward. Let go of the outside world. Experience yourself in the moment.

3 Mentally release the weight of your body. Imagine that your body is melting into the ground. Just let go.

4 Scan your body, feeling the softness in each part: your feet and legs, buttocks, hips, abdomen, chest, shoulders, arms and hands. Feel that your head is balanced. Relax your jaw, soften your whole face. Feel your body.

5 Extend your spine upwards towards the crown of your head. Allow your chest to open at the same time.

6 Feel your whole body with full awareness. Notice any sensations. Accept the way your body is feeling. Remain focused on your body for two to three minutes.

7 Now focus your attention on your breathing. Feel the inhalations and the exhalations. Notice the rhythm of expansion and contraction. Do not interfere with your breathing, just watch it for two to three minutes.

8 Now open your awareness fully to the environment. Notice any aromas, feel the atmosphere around you. Listen to all the sounds, near and far. Pay attention to all external stimuli for two to three minutes.

9 Bring your awareness back to your body. Focus on your breathing. Feel the gentle movement in your chest or notice the movement of air in your nostrils. Feel the rhythm.

10 Expand your awareness and feel your whole body. Feel the quietness and softness. Notice how the breath is moving in your body.

11 Pay attention to your spine, making sure that it is erect. Take a full breath and release it slowly.

12 Start the concentration technique of your choice.

A few simple concentration techniques are described under the heading METHODS OF MEDITATION on page 64.

practice of meditation

There are thousands of different techniques to calm and focus the mind. All of them have one aim: to bring the mind to a still point. Once the mind is quiet and spacious, subtle levels of awareness are able to arise. This is a simple and natural process and therefore the practice of meditation is also very simple.

When we start the practice, we sit quietly and we turn our awareness around; we turn it inwards. Normally we respond to the external stimuli of our environment and we are caught up in continual thought patterns. When we turn inward, we first withdraw from stimulation. We then discover that our minds are never still. In the tradition of meditation we refer to this internal chatter as "monkey mind".

In the beginning, the practice of meditation is nothing more than following a chosen technique to concentrate the mind. It is through the skill of concentration that we gradually train the monkey mind to be quiet and focused. We simply focus the mind on one object and repeatedly bring our awareness back to the point of concentration when the mind wanders off.

Initially it consists of becoming aware: of our thinking, of our letting go of thoughts, of our refocusing on the object of concentration. This simple technique is done with full awareness. We should be fully present, fully focused in each moment. We must "know" that we are thinking, we must "know" that we are letting go, we must "know" that we are refocusing, and we must "know" that we are fully aware in each moment. This is how we cultivate awareness.

It is important that this process is done with detachment. We should not try to force the mind; we should not suppress and we should not manipulate. We should let the mind move freely and allow thoughts to pass through like clouds drifting past in the sky. A relaxed, nonjudgemental attitude is necessary when practising any one of the techniques. If we have certain expectations or if we become emotionally involved with the process to happen, we are not practising meditation. Meditation requires objectivity, patience and acceptance. We should "watch" the process, not control it. We should allow the process, not force it.

It is through repetition that we train the mind. By bringing the mind back again and again to a neutral point of focus the obsessive pattern of the monkey mind is broken. It is because we do not engage in the process that the change happens. Letting go of activity and coming back to a neutral place of stillness actually changes our brain wave patterns.

Regular practice is important. When we start, we should sit for twenty minutes each day, or as often as we are able to. Meditation works cumulatively and even if we just sit down for ten minutes and do some deep breathing, we are gaining benefit.

Early morning or dusk are good times to do our practice, but the important thing is to find a time when we will not be disturbed. It helps a lot to have a quiet, pleasant and private place that we use regularly. If we manage to create a comfortable routine for ourselves, we will find that we practise more regularly. The trick is to make our practice a pleasure, not a duty.

CONCENTRATION ON BREATHING

This is a very simple but effective way to train the mind in concentration. It is essential to breathe through the nose. Both nostrils should be open to allow the breath to flow freely.

1   Find a quiet place where you can sit for 20 or 30 minutes without being disturbed. It is advisable to use the same place every time you do your practice.

2   Take time to do the STILLING AND CENTRING exercise which is described on page 58.

3   When you have completed your preparation, bring your awareness back to your breathing. Do not manipulate or change it in any way. Allow your breath to breathe itself.

4   Focus fully but gently on your breathing. Notice the duration of the inhalations and exhalations. Notice the quality and the texture of your breathing. Notice any differences between the inhalations and exhalations. Notice when the rhythm changes.

5   Your awareness should be finely tuned to your breathing. Bring your mind gently back to this focal point every time it starts to wander.

6   Thoughts, ideas, worries, and fantasies will move into the mind all the time. This is normal. Notice each thought, let go of it and refocus on your breathing. Do not engage with or respond to the thoughts. Remain objective.

7   Your focus on your breathing should be alert but soft. Do not force your mind. Do not change your breathing.

8   The quality of your thoughts may influence the quality of your breathing. Pay attention to the nuances, but do not change what is happening. Your attitude should be passive and detached. Just watch. Do not respond, do not judge.

9   If any one thought becomes obsessive, stay with it for a while. Allow the scenario to unfold and act itself out for a while. Do not engage in it. Come back to your breathing. Feel the rhythm. Notice where the breath is moving. Become aware that your thoughts are creations of your mind, nothing more.

10   Follow this technique for 20 or 30 minutes. Make the transition back into your day gentle. Do not rush back. Pay attention to how you are feeling.

methods of meditation

The many different methods of meditation practice all have a few simple, basic rules that need to be followed:

- we should sit still and be comfortable;
- the body should be relaxed and the spine straight;
- there should be no need to respond to distractions;
- our breathing should be quiet and regular;
- we should concentrate on an object with passive awareness;
- we should have no expectations from our practice.

The choice of the object of concentration is left to personal preference. We can choose a concrete object such as a flower, a dot, or the flame of a candle. Alternatively, we can choose an abstract object such as a sound or an image. Most traditions use breathing as an alternative or primer point of concentration. A focus on breathing anchors the mind in the body and thus contributes to a more holistic experience.

When we use a concrete object, we place it so that the eyes can gently gaze at it while the head is comfortably balanced. The aim of the object is to supply a neutral, visual stimulus for the mind to concentrate on. With softly focused eyes we gaze at the object in a relaxed way for a few minutes. We then close our eyes and view the "afterimage" of the object in our mind's eye. We simply alternate between these two actions, relaxing into the experience.

The technique is the same for an abstract object. A popular choice is to repeat a sound, word or phrase mentally. The meaning may be neutral, sacred or have contemplative associations – it makes no difference. What is important is that the mental repetition must be rhythmical and regular. When an image is chosen, the mind should rest as easily on the image as the eyes would rest on an object.

The object of concentration anchors the mind; it focuses the awareness. Most of the time, however, we will be watching our thoughts and not the object. This is completely normal. The technique is to bring the mind back repeatedly, not to try to have a blank mind. Our minds are busy and creative, which is what they are supposed to be.

Simple, concentrative techniques all work on the same principle: by bringing the mind back to one neutral point over and over, the mental chatter will eventually start to subside. Initially the mind will throw up all our conscious and subconscious preoccupations. This is the process of purification: the release of churning or tightly held thoughts, fantasies, worries and obsessions. When the monkey mind starts to come to rest, we discover a calm spaciousness. This is the natural state of our mind.

Through meditation we are learning to become aware of our thoughts so that we can become more conscious of our mental patterns. We are also bringing calmness and balance to the mental and physical parts of ourselves. The process should not be used to suppress, deny or manipulate an artificial response.

When we sit by ourselves, we often feel as if nothing is happening, as if we are wasting our time. This is never true. Spending some quiet time with ourselves is always meaningful and beneficial. It is also important to learn to trust the process.

CONCENTRATION ON THE STILL POINT

This technique is a follow-up to the CONCENTRA-TION ON BREATHING technique. It can be used in combination with that technique, or on its own.

1 Sit down in your habitual meditation area and settle into your posture. Place a watch or clock in a position where it can easily be seen. Glance at it occasionally to time your practice.

2 Do the STILLING AND CENTRING exercise which is described on page 58.

3 Bring your awareness back to your breathing. Watch your breathing with detached alertness. Follow the same method as described in the CONCENTRATION ON BREATHING technique on page 62.

4 Follow your breathing until it has become calm and regular. Your body, breathing and mind should feel settled and integrated.

5 Focus your awareness on the pause between the out-breath and the following in-breath. Do not change your breathing. Pay attention to the inhalation. Pay attention to the exhalation. Focus on the pause between the two.

6 If the pause is short, allow it to be short. If the pause gets longer, notice the stillness. Feel the stillness in your whole body during the pause.

7 Should the rhythm of your breathing become jerky or irregular, refocus on it. Still point concentration depends on a slow, regular rhythm of breath flow.

8 Should your breathing or your mind feel tight at any time, take a wilfull, deep breath and release it slowly. Check that your spine is erect and that your jaw is relaxed.

9 Refocus on the process of breathing. Relax and let go into the pause. Melt into the pause. Remain attentive to your breathing.

10 Releasing into the still point brings openness to the mind and body. It creates space. Be attentive to the subtle sensations of spaciousness that are cultivated during this practice. Allow them to linger.

lifestyle

Introducing meditation into our lives will slowly but surely start to influence our lifestyle. As our awareness expands, we will start to think and feel differently. When the mind opens up and gains in clarity, the world starts to look like a different place. It is only natural that we find ourselves adjusting values and changing perceptions.

Basically meditation is a process of purification, which helps us to let go and cut through ignorance and negative mind states. A mind that is cluttered with unhealthy thoughts and blocked by anxiety limits our growth. With the unfolding of insight and understanding we manage to see more clearly the areas in our lives that need attention.

We all have dreams and plans to change and improve our lives. Most of us find that our lives are too complicated. Most of us have a tendency to hold on to possessions and relationships. As we grow, however, we find that much of what we are carrying with us has become unnecessary baggage. The need to travel lighter through life introduces a shift towards a less complicated lifestyle.

When we start to cultivate a preference for that which is simple, pure and natural, much of what we have gathered becomes redundant. Clearing out and letting go is a pleasant and positive process; it makes us feel light; it brings a sense of freedom. It creates space.

Mental clarity has a tendency to clear away that which is not serving us any longer. With greater discrimination it becomes possible to make decisions about what is serving our growth and what is blocking us.

Simplicity adds an element of freedom to life. When we start to notice that less may actually mean more, we start to change and we enjoy letting go of that which is unnecessary. This attitude will influence our lifestyle on all levels, from the food that we eat to the way in which we decorate our homes; from the clothes that we wear to the way that we spend our vacations.

Inner purification usually manifests itself in outer simplicity, and simplicity brings us closer to truth. Through finding greater truth we become happier and healthier human beings. Truth is simple; it is whole and it is empowering. It is nonnegotiable; it is the essence of who we are. Finding greater truth in our lives is the path to greater inner balance, to wholeness. It is authentic empowerment.

Through introducing meditation into our lives we are in fact changing the rhythm of our daily routine. A short period of stillness and inner focus becomes part of our day, and this gradually starts to remould our inner rhythm. Our thinking starts to change and also our habitual patterns.

A lifestyle that is shaped by simplicity and truth allows us to live with reverence upon the earth. All life is interrelated and it is through simple living that we can share the abundance of the earth in a natural way.

diet

A basic truth is that we are what we think. With the quality of our thoughts we create our reality. We are what we eat is similarly true. The foods we choose to nourish ourselves with are the building blocks of our bodies. What we eat and drink will directly influence our level of wellbeing.

Bad dietary habits create stress on the physical system and this influences our state of mind. Stimulants such ase coffee and alcohol lead to an imbalance in our autonomic nervous system. The aim of meditation is to bring balance and tranquillity to our nervous system, so it is only natural that we start to cut out toxins and stimulants. It is easier to let go of compulsions and addictions when we feel balanced and calm.

The tendency towards a more balanced lifestyle with healthier eating habits will influence the choices which we make. We will start choosing fish instead of meat, honey instead of sugar, brown rice instead of white, polished rice. Eating from the earth will start making more sense than eating from the factories, and drinking more juice and less alcohol will start to feel good. As our minds and bodies find more equilibrium we will start to eat more fruit and vegetables, we will drink less coffee and we may even decide to challenge the smoking habit.

Taking time to nourish ourselves is an important part of our everyday life. How we eat is as important as what we eat. Mind and body are interrelated and our mental attitude is important. We should be fully present when we eat. It is quite a challenge for most of us to start eating with appreciation and awareness.

Appreciating and enjoying our food contributes to digestion and assimilation. When we start to eat with full awareness, when we start to pay attention to how we nourish ourselves, we will naturally start to eat whole and fresh foods. It just simply feels right to do so.

We gradually become more sensitive to our bodies and we will find that it is not a good idea to meditate after a meal. A body that is over-stimulated, filled with toxins and heavy with digestive overload will not feel comfortable when we meditate. The activity of our circulatory and nervous systems should be focused in the head and not in the abdomen. We want to favour the subtle energies of our awareness, not the gross energies of our body.

Through meditation we gradually bring the mind and body back to a more natural and pure state. Wholeness is a natural way of being, in our bodies as it is in nature. Through wholeness we come into balance, we naturally shift into alignment. This condition changes our inner rhythm. We become calm, balanced and we feel more in harmony with the universe.

As we grow in consciousness, we become more aware of the intimate relationship between the choices we make and our state of well-being. Everything we do results from choice. There is always an option, even if it is only the choice of our attitude. Choosing what to eat and how to enjoy our food is a daily exercise in awareness. It is also a daily reminder of the responsibility we have towards ourselves.

EATING WITH AWARENESS

We eat every day. To bring mindfulness to our eating is an excellent practice in awareness. It is also a good way to slow down our eating patterns. Taking more time with food benefits the digestion.

1 Choose a time when you are alone and when you are not rushed. It may be a mealtime or a time for a snack.

2 Prepare what you are going to eat and place it in front of you. Look at the food. Notice what you are seeing: colour, texture, shape . . .

3 Reach out and bring the food to your mouth. Notice the movement of your hand and arm. Keep your attention focused on the food. Be aware that you are starting the process of eating.

4 Place the food in your mouth. Notice the experiences of smelling, feeling, tasting. Chew slowly and pay attention to the process. Be aware of the different tastes and textures. Experience the process fully.

5 Swallow and pay attention to the aftertaste of the food. Notice the intention that arises to take the next mouthful. Notice your body. Experience your arm reaching out.

6 Bring the next bite to your mouth. Pay attention to the process as you are repeating it. Be aware of each stage and know that you are smelling, biting, feeling, tasting, chewing, swallowing.

7 As you slowly and mindfully continue eating, extend your awareness to the whole of yourself. Feel your whole body. Make sure you are relaxed. Be aware that your body is busy with the process of eating and digesting. You are nourishing yourself.

8 Notice that you are breathing. Pay attention to the rhythm of your breathing. Feel your chest move.

9 Continue eating with full awareness of the food you are enjoying, the air you are breathing and the feelings in your body.

10 When you have finished, reflect for a few minutes before you get up. Notice your feelings.

Eating with awareness can be a daily meditation time for people who do not have any other time to be still.

exercise

Exercise is necessary to maintain a healthy body. A strong, balanced body is important for our growth and development. The mind and body are interrelated and interdependent. If we want to train the mind, grow in awareness and expand our consciousness, we will do well to also keep the body fit.

Being fully present in the body, and having a pain-free and healthy body will greatly enhance our meditation practice. When we sit quietly and focus inward, the body is our first object of attention. We cannot centre ourselves without feeling and paying attention to the body. If the body is tight and uncomfortable our sitting will be an unsettling experience.

Physical training is often part and parcel of a serious programme of self-development. This is because inner growth begins with awareness and self-awareness begins in the body. To know who we are, to get into intimate contact with ourselves, we need to connect with our feelings. Our feelings are all registered in the body. Some are subliminal and some express themselves as body sensations.

What we think is how we create our reality, *how* we feel is how we experience reality. The mind thinks, the body feels. The mind plays games, the body speaks the truth. The body is like a machine, like a computor; what you put in is what you get out. The mind is like a magician; it can change one thing into something else.

To have a pure and supple body is as important as it is to have a clear and trained mind. When the two are synchronised, when both body and mind are finely tuned and in balance, our life experience becomes a joy.

Practices like hatha yoga, t'ai chi and the martial arts contribute to meditation because they develop and coordinate the body and the mind. They were designed to calm the mind, to increase concentration skills and to expand internal awareness. These practices also work with the breath in a very focused and dynamic way. Training and strengthening our body-mind-breath connection is an excellent preparation for meditation practice.

Hatha yoga consists of stretches and held postures, combined with deep, regular breathing. Deep relaxation forms an integral part of most hatha yoga classes. The reason why hatha yoga was developed many thousands of years ago was to prepare the physical vehicle for the practice of meditation. Today this is as true as ever. Meditation after a yoga class is usually a more profound experience.

T'ai chi is regarded as meditation-in-motion because it uses slow, flowing movements to centre awareness. Total concentration is necessary and awareness and control of breathing are indispensable. Strengthening the physical body is as important as the focus and alertness of the mind.

The martial arts cultivate the same qualities as hatha yoga and t'ai chi. Like meditation, we can practise these disciplines on our own with much benefit. However, working in a group with a good teacher will make the experience and the learning much richer.

RELEASING THE SPINE

This is a simple exercise to become aware of the body and its shifting sensations. The head, arms and shoulders are released in a forward-moving motion. The point of gravity within the body changes, the head drops below the heart, and the mind is drawn into an awareness of the body.

1 Stand with your feet hip-width apart, toes pointing forward.

2 Lengthen your spine by extending the crown of your head upwards.

3 Relax your whole body. Gently close your eyes.

4 Take a few slow, deep breaths. Feel your diaphragm extending and your chest opening.

5 Release your jaw, relax your face, neck and shoulders.

6 Roll your head forward and feel the back of your neck opening. Allow your head to keep moving down towards the ground. Release your arms and let them dangle next to your head. Move slowly.

7 Allow your head, arms and shoulders to move slowly down towards the ground. Feel your spine slowly releasing. At the end of the movement, bend your knees and allow your lower back to open more.

8 Let your head, arms and upper torso hang for about 20 seconds. Relax completely. Feel all the sensations.

9 Slowly roll up. Keep your eyes closed. Stand quietly for about ten seconds. Breathe deeply. Feel your body.

This gentle exercise will relax the spine, open the lower back and centre your awareness in your body. It prepares body and mind for meditation.

OPENING THE CHEST

This is a simple breathing and stretching exercise to bring awareness into the chest. Pay attention to the sensations in your torso as you extend and breathe.

1 Stand with your feet hip-width apart. Lengthen your spine by stretching towards the crown of your head.

2 Extend your fingers and sweep your arms up overhead, stretching them towards the sky. Inhale as you move your arms upwards.

3 Breathe out as you sweep your arms down towards your body. Breath and movement must be synchronised.

4 Repeat these movements 5 times, inhaling through your nose, exhaling through your mouth.

5 Now stretch your arms up and interlace your fingers above your head. Stretch up, reach for the sky, feel your chest opening as your arms extend.

6 Inhale. Exhale as you stretch your torso over to the right. Feel the left side of your chest opening. Hold the position for one more deep breath.

7   Come back to the centre. Inhale. Exhale as you stretch over to the left. Hold for one deep breath.

8   Come back to the centre. Repeat 4 times, stretching a little further each time. Feel your body open.

9   Use deep diaphragmatic breaths, inhaling through your nose, exhaling through your mouth. Do not overstretch.

This exercise prepares the body for meditation by energising and opening up the torso. It stretches and expands the ribcage and the diaphragm. It releases the shoulders and lower back.

"The explanations for the development of disease that science provides are essential, but they are insufficient. We live now in a society deeply alive psychologically, in which millions of individuals are putting serious effort into understanding their inner selves."
– *Caroline Myss*

"Since it is the self by which we suffer, so it is the self by which we will find relief."
– *Upanishads*

"We believe that each person directly participates, either consciously or unconsciously, in the creation of his or her own reality, including the reality of their health. The tools that we use in the process of this creation reside within us. They are our attitudes, emotions and belief patterns as well as an awareness of our spiritual self."
– *Caroline Myss*

"Relaxation is not something that you do. It is a natural response that you allow to happen. Relaxation is what is left when you stop creating tension."
– *J. and M. Levey*

stress

We are all familiar with the fight-or-flight response. These are the arousal symptoms that the body produces when we experience crises or trauma. The blood pressure shoots up, the heart starts to pound, breathing becomes fast and shallow, the muscles tense up and the palms become sweaty.

Humans and animals alike can create super power and endurance in their bodies when they are fighting for survival. Physiologically we are exquisitely equipped to cope with all that life brings us.

In direct contrast to the fight-or-flight response, we have the relaxation response. The most important features of this state are:

- the heart rate decreases and the blood pressure drops;
- the rate of breathing and of oxygen consumption decreases;
- blood flow to the muscles decreases and flows instead to the brain and the skin;
- brain waves shift from an alert beta rhythm to a relaxed alpha rhythm.

All forms of meditation induce the relaxation response. This is the most basic way in which we benefit from it. Sitting still and turning the focus inward changes the chemistry of the physical body. However, the benefits go far beyond this response.

Stress is a natural part of life. Where there are polarities, there is

tension, and where there is tension, there is stress. The challenge is not to eliminate stress, but it is how to manage it in a mature way. When we use the mind as a stress-management tool, we develop the ability to use the mental energy aroused by stress in a creative way.

If this is not possible, we have another choice: to change the quality of our mental energy by changing our perception. In this way we neutralise the harmful and dysfunctional stress patterns that our minds are creating. We are on this earth to learn, to evolve, not to change the world when it is not to our liking.

Unhealthy stress creates imbalances in the form of psychosomatic disorders. Psyche means mind and soma means body. These disorders thus originate in the mind and manifest in the body. When we take drugs, we are suppressing the physical symptoms and are not changing the cause of the problem. Suppressing symptoms is an unhealthy and irresponsible way of coping with stress.

All stress-related disorders will improve if we let go of the tightness in our minds. Our minds are consciously and unconsciously holding on to conditioned mind states. We have fixed opinions and we carry certain expectations. These mind sets create a tight, unbending mental attitude. This is where the stress originates – in our minds, not in the outside world. Learning to go with the flow of life is a major step forward in eliminating unnecessary stress.

With maturity we learn to understand and accept; we learn that our challenge is to flow with life, not to try to change it. Nobody trains us in growing up, in developing wisdom. This is just simply not part of the normal curriculum. Meditation brings maturity to the mind. Awareness and insight build a mature mental attitude which is the natural and most effective way of coping with stress.

"When the mind has settled, we are established in our essential nature, which is unbounded Consciousness."
– *Patanjali*

"A conscious lifetime is a treasure beyond value."
– *Gary Zukav*

"Evolution does not lie in becoming more and more saintly or more and more intelligent, but more and more conscious . . . "
– *Aurobindo*

"What consciousness means is that you are choosing to become personally aware of exactly where your spirit goes . . . "
– *Caroline Myss*

"Light and consciousness share several things in common. One of them concerns a central thread of our exploration – the present moment."
– *Peter Russell*

"The Light that flows through your system is Universal energy. It is the Light of the Universe . . . What you feel, what you think, how you behave . . . reflect the way that you are shaping the Light that is flowing through you . . . You change the way that you shape the Light which is flowing through you by changing your consciousness."
– Gary Zukav

"Our normal waking consciousness is but one special type of consciousness, while all about it parted from it by the filmiest of screens there lie potential forms of consciousness entirely different. We may go through life without suspecting their existence, but apply the requisite stimulus and at a touch they are there in all their completeness . . . ."
– William James

conciousness

Who we are, how we function and how we create the quality of our life are all products of our consciousness. This is who we are: we are our consciousness. We are this radiance which animates our innermost essence.

Being conscious means being fully awake. It means being fully aware of our thinking and feeling, of our sensing and intuiting. The more conscious we are, the sharper and finer these abilities will function. A highly conscious person is more evolved than a relatively conscious person – such a person will be more whole, more radiant, more mature, and will relate to life in a more responsible way. We are all progressing on this upward spiral.

The upward spiral into more subtle levels of consciousness is what our personal process of evolution is all about. This is the goal and meaning of meditation. By turning our attention inward, we start to become aware of ourselves in new ways.

Expanding consciousness is a gradual process of waking up to new ways of thinking and feeling, fuller ways of sensing, and finer ways of intuiting. The different areas of consciousness are all interrelated and interdependent in a holistic way. In order to grow into healthy, whole human beings, we need to develop in a balanced way. Taking responsibility for this process is our personal challenge.

Because of different belief systems we relate to this challenge in different ways. For some of us this process is only relevant for one lifetime. For others, the process spans a succession of lifetimes because of a belief in reincarnation. It matters not how we see it, what matters is how we manage to grow in this present life of ours. Taking responsibility for our self-development from day to day, from year to year, is important.

Life is a process. How we relate to this process, how we take responsibility for our self-development, directly influences the flowering of our consciousness. Nature will move us along, but we are the architects of our personal process.

At first we are involved with sorting out our survival issues, our physical security in this world. This starts to unfold our self-consciousness. We then need to come to grips with the issues of external power: sex, money and relationships. These power issues as well as our sense of self become the areas in which we continue to mould our consciousness. It is a natural process of maturation.

As we mature, our perceptions of love and will start to evolve. Unconditional love and the acceptance of divine will begin to filter through. Eventually wisdom and the subtle awareness of the oneness of all creation expand our consciousness further.

On each level of development we need to integrate our experiences and our understanding before we move on. Before we can integrate a process in a meaningful way, all the necessary elements need to be present and this requires awareness. Meditation cultivates awareness. This is how we contribute to our upward movement on the spiral of consciousness: we cultivate awareness.

"It is the health of the soul that is the true purpose of the human experience. Everything serves that."
– *Gary Zukav*

"Spiritual growth consists in weakening our identification with our small selves in order to achieve divine awareness."
– *Wendlyn Alter*

"The vertical path is the path of awareness. It is the path of consciousness and conscious choice. The person who chooses to advance his or her spiritual growth, to cultivate awareness of his or her higher self, is on a vertical path."
– *Gary Zukav*

"The most beautiful thing we can experience is the mystery."
– *Albert Einstein*

"The best decisions are not made with the head. Still your mind, open your heart, and let them come from a level even deeper than the heart."
– *Aruna Bhargava*

spirituality

The notion that meditation is a form of religion is incorrect. What is true, however, is that many religions use the technique of meditation for spiritual practice. Eastern religions and the mystical paths of all Western religions accept meditation and contemplative prayer as powerful methods to transcend the self and to reach higher states of consciousness.

Deep meditation slows down the activities of the mind and prolonged periods of meditation purify negative mind states. Such a mind is open, and the spacious quality invites more subtle areas of consciousness to unfold. This is the path to an illumined mind; it is the process of becoming more enlightened.

Through the ages, saints, sages and mystics of all traditions have used meditation and contemplation in some form or other to enhance their spiritual practice. All forms of meditation bring us closer to our spiritual essence. Our spiritual awareness grows when we start to understand that we are spiritual beings and that we are thus connected to all of creation.

When we experience reverence for all life, when we honour our interrelatedness, we are having a spiritual experience, not a religious one. Religions divide us, spirituality unites us. Religions are based on dogma; spirituality honours all life as spirit.

A religion is a particular system of worshipping a higher power; it is the way we choose to express our faith in God. Spirituality is

acknowledging the vital animating essence of ourselves. It is honouring our souls, the immortal part of ourselves, as an integral part of all creation. Spirituality is beyond religion because it means unification, it means one spirit, one energy, one breath. It means an ever-expanding progression towards oneness, towards the ultimate Source which people call by different names: God, Allah, Yahweh, Brahman, Absulute Mind, Pure Consciousness.

God-honouring traditions use different forms of meditation or contemplation to enhance their worship and to express their devotion. The prayer of the heart, centring prayer, devotional chanting, ritualistic practices and repetitive body movements are all forms of centring awareness and stilling the mind. These forms of worship open the devotee to experiencing God in a direct way. During these practices there is a drawing in of energy from the Divine Source.

Meditation does for the mind what food does for the body; it nourishes it and it stimulates growth. Our bodies need to grow from being small, vulnerable babies into becoming strong, healthy adults, while our minds need to develop from unconsciousness to consciousness. Nourishing the mind through meditation will first bring basic benefits such as relaxation and concentration, later it will bring awareness and greater insight and much later it could bring illumination.

These are all areas of consciousness that unfold as we evolve. Meditation can bring more light to the mind, which is why all traditions honour it as a practice. It is a path to Enlightenment.

"One does not become enlightened by imagining figures of light, but by making the darkness conscious."
– *Carl Jung*

"If each of us can believe, that he is working so that the Universe may be raised, in him and through him, to a higher level, then a new spring of energy will well forth in the heart of Earth's workers."
– *Teilhard de Chardin*

"A vital aspect of the enlightened state is the experience of an all-pervading unity. 'This' and 'that' no longer are separate entities. They are different forms of the same thing."
– *Gary Zukav*

"It is a kind of mystery that for people who have no experience of enlightenment, enlightenment is something wonderful. But if they attain it, it is nothing. But yet it is not nothing. Do you understand?"
– *Shunryu Suzuki*

"There is Light, and there is the shaping of Light by consciousness. This is creation."
– *Gary Zukav*

"A nice definition of an awakened person: a person who no longer marches to the drums of society, a person who dances to the tune of the music that springs up from within."
– *Anthony de Mello*

enlightenment

The aim of meditation is to transform consciousness. Consciousness is a state of being; we experience it, we are it. It has no form; it cannot be measured. It can however be expressed. All forms of life express consciousness. We have reached a stage in our evolution where we are starting to recognise that consciousness is the essence of all life.

There are many different ways in which consciousness manifests itself. The spectrum is large, the manifestations are innumerable. The metaphor which is commonly used for human consciousness is light. We relate to consciousness in the same way as we understand the properties of light: the brighter the light, the higher the frequency of its vibration – the finer the consciousness, the more radiant the consciousness. The lower the frequency of the vibration, the less light there will be – the denser the consciousness, the less radiance there will be.

As we evolve, our consciousness transforms to higher frequencies of vibrations. This can be sensed as a process of growing more and more into light. As we become less dense and more light, as we become less fragmented and more radiant, we become more conscious. This is the process of en-light-enment.

Like meditation, enlightenment is an ongoing process. It is a natural process of gradual transformation. We cannot do it, we cannot get it, we cannot achieve it. As we practise the art of conscious living, we evolve into it. In a natural way, we are all busy with the process of enlightenment, every one of us. Meditation assists this process.

All spiritual traditions focus on the growth towards greater light. The unfolding of personal consciousness is seen as the inner light, or consciousness, of the individual merging with the source of all light. In the West we refer to the source as Christ consciousness, while those in the East relate to Cosmic Consciousness.

In Eastern spiritual traditions, enlightenment is called different names by the different traditions, because the nature of the training differs as well as the enlightened state that is being cultivated. The yoga traditions prepare the aspirants for *samadhi,* the Buddhists seek *nirvana* and Zen aims at *kensho* or *satori.*

In the West, mystics, artists and visionaries also experience higher states of consciousness in a variety of ways. The expression of these illumined states reflects the particular background and disposition of the individuals. What they all have in common, however, is the experience of oneness, the merging with a higher, brighter state of consciousness.

Growing more and more into light, becoming more conscious, more radiant, is the natural path of our evolution. This is our purpose for being here. We are spiritual beings and we have reached the stage in our evolution as a species where we are becoming conscious of our spiritual destiny. By taking responsibility for our lives in a full and inspired way, we are able to assist the process of our evolution. Meditation is one of the most powerful techniques to assist us on this journey.

"A man does not seek to see himself in running water, but in still water. For only what is itself still can impart stillness to others."
– *Chuang-Tse*

"We have what we seek. It is there all the time, and if we give it time it will make itself known to us."
– *Thomas Merton*

"The more and more you listen, the more and more you will hear. The more you hear, the more and more deeply you will understand."
– *Khyentse Rinpoche*

"Nothing in all creation is so like God as silence."
– *Meister Eckhart*

"The more you talk about it, and the more you think about it, the further from it you go. Stop talking. Stop thinking, and there is nothing you will not understand."
– *Seng-Ts'an*

retreat

Going on retreat is an intentional decision to withdraw temporarily from the action and demands of daily living. It is an opportunity to centre ourselves, and to renew our sense of who we are and how we are living our life. A retreat is a time to let go, to allow ourselves to open up, and to refocus.

People go on retreat for different reasons. Some need to let go of stress and anxiety. Some need space and time to sort out problems and inner turmoil. Others are on a spiritual journey and are seeking an opportunity for inward exploration. The common need is to get away from the habitual stimuli to which we are normally exposed. When we go on retreat we are seeking outer stillness to enable us to find some inner stillness.

We are living in challenging times. Most of us are finding it necessary to restructure our lives. We need time and space to reflect. A retreat enables us to get away from sensory overload and continual mental performance. It is a place of quiet where the emphasis is on silence, simplicity and meditation. These are excellent tools for stimulating inner consciousness.

Stillness and inner focus allow the body, the mind and the soul to come to a place of rest, to soften, to open up. Letting go of tightness stimulates growth; it allows energy to flow. The retreat experience may be one of greater spiritual awareness or simply a sense of well-being. But it will be an experience of cleansing and energising and of feeling more positively engaged with life.

Expanding consciousness implies the unfolding of our potential. It means becoming more than we already are. When we are active in the material world, we develop external consciousness. To be successful we need to be alert, smart and awake. Our awareness of external situations needs to be sharp. If we are not fully conscious of the stimuli around us, we will often fall short.

Internal consciousness demands that we are aware of our internal world. This is the world of intuition, of wisdom, of truth, of compassion. It is the world of our soul. Care of the soul asks that we pay attention to our spiritual needs. When we are balancing the needs of our spiritual world with the demands of our material world, we are living in harmony with ourselves. When we do not achieve this balance, we will experience stress, depression or some kind of anxiety.

A retreat is always designed to bring rest, balance, inspiration and spiritual renewal. A peaceful environment, relaxation and breathing exercises, contemplation and meditation – these are the inner techniques for bringing about change. The outer methods are physical exercise, body therapies like aromatherapy or shiatsu, and a cleansing diet. There are different kinds of retreats. Most of them will use a combination of these practices.

Going on retreat is a holistic experience. We focus on body, mind and soul and we bring them into alignment. We also bring our outer world into balance with our inner world. When we align our physical reality with our spiritual reality, we empower ourselves. A balanced, fully aware individual is an empowered human being.

wisdom

Through the purification process of meditation we discover the true power of our inner wisdom. Wisdom is a natural attunement to the laws of the universe. It is natural to be able to distinguish between that which is bad from that which is good. It is natural to understand that love draws goodness towards you and that hate creates negative responses. We all have wisdom; it is within our nature.

We are living through times of profound transformation. The needs of our country can best be served by people of wisdom. Through wisdom we access parts of ourselves that enrich us and that empower us for the work we need to do. Honesty, courage and compassion come into focus through wisdom. These are powerful tools for managing change and transformation.

Through the quality of honesty we access truth. Truth helps us to see more clearly and to clear away personal prejudice. To see our world as it really is, not as we wish to see it, needs honesty. The truth is that we as human beings all have the same needs, the same joys and the same pains. We need to accept our interrelatedness and our interdependence with honesty and courage.

Courage to do what is right, courage to accept the basic truths of life willingly is available to all of us. Courage is part of the human condition. Through wisdom we learn to apply our courage to the full spectrum of our experiences. Having the courage to let go of the unnecessary things that we are holding on to needs wisdom.

"It is the present, not the past – not our history – that holds the key to the character of the future."
– *David Spangler*

"If we are to continue our evolutionary journey it is imperative that we now make some equally prodigious leaps in consciousness. We must develop the wisdom that will allow us to use new powers for our own good – and for the good of all. This is the challenge of our times."
– *Peter Russell*

"Truth is that which does not contaminate you, but empowers you . . .
We need truth to grow in the same way that we need vitamins, affection and love."
– *Gary Zukav*

"When a man gains victory over himself, the unfolding of love is possible."
– *Rudolf Steiner*

Compassion is the courage of the mind to follow the heart. It allows the heart to open and to respond with the deepest truth from within ourselves. When we can accept our mistakes, face our vulnerability and open up to compassion, we can transform ourselves and our world. Compassion is kindness of the heart. Compassion is born from knowing that we are all one, that when we are doing unto others as we would they do unto us, we are accepting the interrelatedness of all life.

All human beings carry within themselves the basic need to do good. Like our wisdom, our basic goodness is always available to us. Through goodwill we radiate the highest part of ourselves and we touch that same place in others. Goodwill is one of the powerful forces that holds the universe together. It is one of the forces that is holding our country together.

When we experience a need to do good to others, we are at the same time expressing goodwill towards ourselves. When we treat others with compassion, we are at the same time expressing compassion towards ourselves. We are all interconnected. Our thoughts, our feelings, our speech and our actions influence not only ourselves but those around us. The vibrations of our electromagnetic field are not confined to our own aura. When we express goodwill, our vibrations reverberate far beyond our physical presence.

Goodwill and compassion flow from an open heart. Insight and understanding flow from a pure mind. When we grow in wisdom, we develop the ability to bring the heart and the mind into harmony. This is how we expand our consciousness; this is how we evolve into more wiser, more empowered human beings.

We are participating in a challenging process. All of us are contributing to the transformation of our country. We are changing from

isolation and enforced separateness to openness and interconnectedness. This is a difficult process. With wisdom we can better manage this transformation.

It is through wisdom that we cultivate authentic power. It is through the grace of wisdom that we gradually align our personalities with our soul. This is how we mature. This is how we develop courage, honesty, compassion and goodwill. This is how we become whole.

Through bringing ourselves into alignment, we become self-empowered human beings. This is the only way in which we can fully and effectively serve our community, our country and the world. When we are serving with the fullness of who we are, we are fulfilling our life's purpose.

suggested further reading

Cooper, David A. – *The Heart of Stillness. The elements of spiritual discipline.* Bell Tower, New York, 1992
– *Silence, Simplicity and Solitude. A guide for spiritual retreat.* Bell Tower, New York, 1992

Dass, Ram – *Journey of Awakening. A meditator's guidebook.* Bantam Books, New York, 1990 (revised edition)

De Mello, Anthony – *Awareness. The perils and opportunities of reality.* Doubleday, New York, 1990
– *Sadhana, a way to God. Christian exercises in Eastern form.* Doubleday, New York, 1984

Easwaran, Eknath – *Meditation. Commonsense directions for an uncommon life.* Arkana, London, 1986

Ferrucci, Piero – *Inevitable Grace. Breakthroughs in the lives of great men and women: Guides to your self-realization.* A Jeremy P. Tarcher/ Putnam Book, New York, 1990

Fontana, David – *The Meditator's Handbook. A comprehensive guide to Eastern and Western meditation techniques.* Element, London, 1992

Griffiths, Bede – *A New Vision of Reality. Western science, Eastern mysticism and Christian faith*. Indus, New Delhi, 1995
– *Return to the Centre*. Indus, New Delhi, 1995

Gunaratana, Ven. Henepola – *Mindfulness in Plain English*. Wisdom Publications, Boston, 1993

Harvey, Andrew – *The Essential Mystics. The soul's journey into truth*. Harper, San Francisco, 1996

Hayward, Jeremy – *Sacred World. A guide to Shambhala warriorship in daily life*. Rider, London, 1995

Housden, Roger – *Retreat. Time apart for silence and solitude*. Thorsons, London, 1995

James, William – *The Varieties of Religious Experience. A study in human nature*. Macmillan Publishing Company, New York, 1985

Jung, Carl G. – *Psychology and the East*. Ark Paperbacks, London, 1978

Kabat-Zinn, Jon – *Wherever You Go, There You Are. Mindfulness meditation in everyday life*. Hyperion, New York, 1994

Keating, Thomas – *Open Mind Open Heart. The contemplative dimension of the Gospel*. Continuum, New York, 1995
– *Intimacy with God. Transformation through contemplation*. Crossroad, New York, 1995

Kornfield, Jack – *A Path with Heart. A guide through the perils and promises of spiritual life.* Bantam Books, New York, 1993

Goldstein, Joseph and Jack Kornfield – *Seeking the Heart of Wisdom. The path of insight meditation.* Shambala, Boston, 1987

Merton, Thomas – *No Man Is an Island.* Burns & Oates, Kent, 1993
– *Contemplation in a World of Action.* Doubleday, New York, 1973

Mitchell, Stephen – *The Enlightened Mind. An anthology of sacred prose* edited by Stephen Mitchell. Harper Collins, New York, 1991
– *The Enlightened Heart. An anthology of sacred poetry.* Harper & Row, New York, 1989

Moacanin, Radmila – *Jung's Psychology and Tibetan Buddhism. Western and Eastern paths to the heart.* Wisdom Publication, Boston, 1986

Myss, Caroline – *Anatomy of the Spirit. The seven stages of power and healing.* Harmony Books, New York, 1996

Nairn, Rob – *Tranquil Mind. An introduction to Buddhism and meditation.* Carrefour/Dragon, Cape Town, 1993

Nhat Hanh, Thich – *Living Buddha, Living Christ. A revered meditation master explores two of the world's great contemplative traditions.* Rider, London, 1995
– *Miracle of Mindfulness.* Beacon, Boston, 1984

Rinpoche, Sogyal – *The Tibetan Book of Living and Dying*. *A new spiritual classic from one of the foremost interpreters of Tibetan Buddhism to the West*. Rider, London, 1992

Suzuki, Shunryu – *Zen Mind, Beginner's Mind*. *Informal talks on Zen meditation and practice*. Weatherhill, New York, 1994

Trungpa, Chögyam – *Shambhala. The sacred path of the warrior*. Shambhala Publications, Boston, 1988
– *Cutting Throuth Spiritual Materialism*. Shambhala Publications, Boston, 1988

Wilber, Ken – *The Spectrum of Consciousness*. *The twentieth anniversary edition of a transpersonal psychology classic*. Quest Books, USA, 1993
– *The Atman Project. A transpersonal view of human development*. Quest Books, USA, 1989

Zukav, Gary – *The Seat of The Soul. An inspiring vision of humanity's spiritual destiny*. Rider, London, 1990

acknowledgements

I wish to acknowledge the work and vision of two people, Gary Zukav and Horace Briel. Both have had a formative influence on my thinking and both have contributed to my growth and to my understanding of conciousness.

Although this a very basic book, it has been a challenge to find ways of simplifying complicated ideas and profound truths. Meditation and conciousness are at the same time simple and complex. Both Gary Zukav and Horace Briel have helped me to find vocabulary to express my ideas clearly.

From Gary Zukav I borrowed directly the phrases "external power" and "authentic power", as well as his expression "aligning the personality with the soul".

Zukav and Briel are both forward thinkers, they have the ability to see beyond the physical world and they both found a profoundly meaningful synthesis between Eastern philopsophy and Western thinking.

Gary Zukav lives in California. His two books, *The Dancing Wu Li Masters* and *The Seat of the Soul* have inspired thousands of people to transform their lives. Horace Briel lives in Cape Town. He works with astrology in a unique way, guiding people in their quest to higher conciousness.